Webinar Domination

Marketing with Webinars

[O. Addey]

Copyright © 2021 **O. Addey**

All rights reserved.

Table of Contents

Introduction 6
Chapter-01: Webinar Domination 7
   What's a Webinar? 7
   What's Webinar Marketing? 7
   How to Build a Webinar 8
      Pick a Popular Topic 8
      Make a Landing Page 9
Chapter-02: How to Choose a Webinar Platform 11
   How To Run a Webinar? 11
      Plan 12
   Choose your platform 13
   Create your content 13
   Promote, promote, promote 14
      Email 15
      Social media 15
      Paid Search 15
      Blogs 15
   Follow-up 16
Chapter-03: Webinar Promotion 17
   Write Helpful Blog Posts 17
   Make Informative Videos 17
   Use Your Email Signature 18
   Leverage social media 18
   Paid Advertisements 19

- How Long Should You Promote a Webinar? 19
- Create a plan for your webinar 20
- Offer your products or services 21
- Pick a webinar software or tool 21

Chapter-04: Benefits of hosting a webinar 23
- You expand your reach 23
- You establish authority in your industry 24
- You save money 24
- You build brand awareness 24
- Webinars help you with market research 25
- Webinars boost sales 26
- Steps to follow when planning a webinar 26
- Get to know your audience 26
- Select your topic 27
- Set a proper date and time for your webinar 28
- Choose your webinar team 28
- Determine the format of your webinar 29
- Recruit speakers for your webinar 29
- Consider your webinar's design and visual branding 29

Chapter-05: WordPress webinar plugins 31
- Ready to Host Your First Webinar? 32
- How to create a perfect webinar 32
- Set your goals 32
- Follow the plan 33
- Hit the perfect time 33

Open for new audiences 34
Spread the news 34
Stick to the script 34
Be technically ready 35
Engage your audience 35
Practice making it (almost) perfect 36
Chapter-06: How to run global webinars? 37
Determine the purpose of your webinar 37
Understand what is required to launch a webinar 38
Decide on your webinar's format 40
    Generate more leads 40
Increase website conversion rates 41
Make your webinar more interactive 42
Practice makes perfect 43
Conclusion 44

Introduction

Business owners who used to meet in person are increasingly relocating to work from home. Meetings are being held online at an unprecedented pace. Zoom user rates alone increased dramatically, with the firm acquiring 2.22 million active users by February of this year. To emphasize the significance of this increase, Zoom only added 1.99 million users in 2019. You are not alone if you have been frantically trying to shift almost every element of your business online. The good news is that software firms are eager to support smooth internet business operations. Are you seeking fresh marketing tactics for your company? What about a marketing approach that can generate high-quality leads in less than an hour? If it seems too good to be true, you haven't heard of webinar marketing. This successful marketing strategy will generate a constant flow of leads for months or years to come with a little commitment of a few hours and minimal money.

Chapter-01: Webinar Domination

What's a Webinar?

A webinar is an online presentation that provides value to your target audience to achieve a certain objective. The phrase webinar is a combination of web and seminar and refers to online training. Marketing webinars help firms capture the attention of their target audience. Because of the power of images, this type of lead creation is more engaging and fascinating than other marketing approaches. We've put up this handy guide to assist you in utilizing the benefits of webinar marketing for the success of your business.

What's Webinar Marketing?

Webinar marketing is the process of promoting a webinar to achieve your company's objectives. You can produce an educational and entertaining webinar, but you will not reap any advantages if no one knows about it. With good webinar marketing, you may achieve a variety of objectives, including:

- Establishing your company's authority
- Creating an email list
- Introducing new services or goods
- Increasing brand awareness

- Putting your company's skills on display

How to Build a Webinar

Because of the perceived challenges, business owners frequently shun webinar marketing. In addition, writing, planning, and creating a webinar may appear to be demanding and time-consuming tasks. However, you have the knowledge and abilities as an expert in your industry to create an instructive webinar from which people may benefit. Here are some suggestions for webinar topics to get you started:

- Extend on previous blog articles
- Consider the recommendations of your audience.
- Go into deeper detail about popular videos.
- Visit the forums that your target audience frequents.
- Break down the webinar-creation process to make it easy to understand.
- Examine the material that your rivals are creating.

Pick a Popular Topic

Finding a fantastic topic is the first step in creating a webinar. It is critical to choose a topic that is relevant to both your target market and audience. For example, if you provide staff management software to small firms, you might hold a webinar that provides entrepreneurs with a hiring guide. Consider frequent queries, pain areas, and issues that your target consumer may encounter. As an industry leader, you can give an explanation or solution to these concerns.

Make a Landing Page

A landing page is a single webpage to which consumers are sent after clicking on one of your promotional links. This website serves as a funnel via which you may take interested people and persuade them to sign up for your webinar. Begin by locating a trustworthy hosting company that provides fast loading speeds and continuous uptime. A fast and responsive landing page is critical for convincing people to attend your next webinar. Your landing page should also include the following elements:

- A description of what your webinar includes Mobile compatibility
- A rallying cry
- Create a Webinar Format
- Your contact details
- Previous customer feedback

When creating a webinar, planning is essential. You don't want to make stuff up as you go. Changes made at the last minute will appear unorganized, unprofessional, and even lazy. Here's an example of a webinar schedule:

- Overview of the subject
- Introductions of the presenters
- Discuss what viewers will discover.

- More information
- Section with questions and answers
- The primary presentation

The major part of the webinar is sandwiched between introduction elements and a breakdown segment. So while the primary presentation is the main attraction and should take up most of your webinar, you don't want to go immediately into it.

Chapter-02: How to Choose a Webinar Platform

Now that you've created an outline for your webinar, it's time to select a platform. If you're familiar with the fundamentals and don't want to pay any money, consider one of these free platforms:

1) Google Hangouts
2) Facebook
3) YouTube

All of these systems provide Livestream or videoconferencing tools that enable basic webinar functionality. However, if you want a specialized webinar platform with more features, you will need to pay some money. Consider the following effective solutions and their highlights:

How To Run a Webinar?

Webinars are not a new technology, but with the current COVID epidemic and lockdown measures, an increasing number of companies are resorting to webinars to connect with their prospects, customers, workers, and the general public. As a result of the growing interest in hosting webinars, many people who have never done a webinar are now expected to develop, arrange, and run one. It's not a simple process! When holding a webinar, several factors to consider, including the content, advertising, platform, and everything in between. It might be a little overwhelming at times. That is why we have compiled a list of 5 easy procedures for hosting a successful webinar (or webinars).

Plan

The first step in running a good webinar is to plan it, and I don't simply mean the material. We prefer to think of a webinar campaign as a sprint, and to be successful in that sprint, and you must have a solid strategy to follow. The first step is to establish a goal. What do you hope to achieve with your webinar? It is critical to respond to this question since it will influence everything else. Do you generate leads? Is your webinar mostly for brand awareness? Is it possible that it is to make income through sponsorship? Once you've determined your aim, you can begin to fill out the remainder of your strategy. Once you've got this, you can start working on the more concrete parts of your webinar.

- What format will the webinar take – live, simulated, or on-demand?
- Who will be your speakers?
- What day and hour will your webinar be held?
- What kind of engagement tools will you employ?

Identifying your audience is a crucial step in addressing these concerns. I don't mean you need particular names, but audience research is an important part of creating a successful webinar program. If you don't know your audience, it's hard to build a content experience that will engage them.

Choose your platform

Not every webinar platform is made equal. Several significant differences may make hosting a certain sort of webinar challenging on one platform but relatively simple on the other. Not all webinar platforms, for example, can perform real simulated webinars in which you may blend a pre-recorded presentation with a live Q&A. This is a crucial feature to have if your objective is to create leads while maximizing ROI.

We've already discussed what questions to ask when investigating webinar platforms, but the essential lesson is to ensure they provide the features you want at a price you're prepared to pay. Then, once you've figured out the features and found a platform that works for you, you can start working on your webinar.

Create your content

When I mention content in this article, I mean your webinar pages, such as the registration page, thank you page, auditorium, and so on.

Because your material is what your audience will interact with, this is the essential element of your pre-webinar effort. Is the content on your webinar pages branded and engaging? Do they provide details about the webinar and your speakers? Then there's the webinar material itself. If you're utilizing a slide presentation, proper practices should be followed here. The most important thing to remember is that less is more! There is a reason why it has become a cliche. You do not need to copy and paste your whole script onto your slides. Instead, choose keywords or images that will help your speakers convey their points.

Also, remember that you do not have to rely just on PowerPoint. Several creative methods generate entertaining webinar material, including movies, animations, GIFs, and even webcams. Consider your personality and what would most likely resonate with your target audience. Regardless of the sort of material you pick, writing it out is critical. This will keep your presenters on track and offer you fantastic information to use when advertising your webinar.

Promote, promote, promote

Nothing is more frustrating than putting in the time and effort to organize a webinar only to have no one show up on the day. No matter how carefully you plan your demographics, they will not appear until you have a complete promoting strategy in place.

The most crucial thing to remember is that your advertising strategy should be multi-channel. You will not reach a large number of people if you only use one or two channels. If you're not sure how to market your webinar or where to promote it, here are some options:

Email

If you have a strong contact list, this will be your primary source of attendance. You should send out an initial invitation and then follow up with non-openers three to four times. And don't forget to send an invite on the day of your webinar properly - same-day invites result in a 20% boost in registrants at WorkCast.

Social media

This is an excellent approach to generate interest in your webinar. We have the best success with webinar registrants on Twitter, Linked In, and Facebook. You could even wish to invest in sponsored social marketing to boost your exposure.

Paid Search

PPC is a fantastic channel to employ, particularly if you want to create new leads. Just make sure you conduct the necessary keyword research to ensure you're bidding on the correct keywords for your event.

Blogs

Blogs are at the heart of any successful inbound marketing effort. They are an excellent method to increase organic traffic and establish oneself as a thought leader. Consider creating blogs about similar themes in the lead-up to your webinar, and then include CTAs in your blog linking to your webinar registration. When it comes to promotion, you should begin at least four weeks before your live webinar date.

Follow-up

Following up with missed webinar attendees and registrants ensures that they remain engaged with your content and brand. It keeps them toasty, as our sales team loves to remark. And a warm lead is far more likely to convert, whether it's to attend another webinar or purchase your goods. Sending out the on-demand recording and a post-event survey can suffice as a follow-up. Alternatively, you may develop a custom file that you email to them later to keep them engaged in the topic. You may even have your new business team contact attendees personally, but depending on the sort of webinar you conducted, this may come off as a bit forceful. Balance is essential here, so make sure that any follow-up you perform is valuable to you and your audience. Running a webinar might be intimidating, but it doesn't have to be difficult. You'll be well on your way to hosting a successful webinar in no time if you follow these instructions.

Chapter-03: Webinar Promotion

Following the completion of your webinar, the emphasis switches to promotion. You must promote this marketing approach to potential consumers for it to be effective. Let's look at some effective webinar marketing techniques for increasing the exposure of your webinar.

Write Helpful Blog Posts

A widely read newsletter or blog is an excellent resource for your webinar marketing strategy. By delivering useful information, you've already established an engaged target audience through various channels. Because your webinar covers comparable themes, your blog readers are an ideal audience to pitch to. While you may openly mention the webinar, people are more responsive when it is less obvious. You may incorporate links to your landing page within your blog entries and mention them at the end of each one. Just be careful not to let this marketing overshadow what your viewers like about your material.

Make Informative Videos

Incorporate information about your next webinar into your normal videos if your company currently utilizes video marketing. The audience watching your videos has already indicated a preference for visual material. Because of the similar setup, they are more likely to be interested in participating in a webinar. The technique is similar to that of blog articles in that you are looking for appropriate locations to mention the webinar.

Use Your Email Signature

You're already in contact with dozens of potential consumers if the typical person sends 128 emails each day. A link in your email signature is a great way to push your webinar to that untapped group gently. In addition, you will spread the news about your webinar without having to do any extra work. It is also less obnoxious than direct email marketing.

Gmail and Outlook, for example, allow users to personalize and include links in their email signatures.

Leverage social media

Social media is a critical component of any webinar marketing plan. These platforms are ideal for disseminating information to a large number of people.

Share a link to your webinar on your page and encourage people to share it if you have a large and engaged following. While sharing may not be as effective for people with lesser social media followings, it does not rule out the use of social media entirely. For example, influencer marketing is a technique that allows you to harness the reach of more popular pages. In a nutshell, you're paying to have a well-known profile advertise your webinar link to attract more traffic than you could with your profile. Because of their link-sharing features, LinkedIn, Facebook, and Twitter are your go-to platforms.

Paid Advertisements

Paid advertising is one of the most dependable kinds of webinar marketing. Because of their remarkable targeting capabilities, Facebook and Google are two of the most potent ad platforms. You may market directly to a target group that is most likely interested in your webinar. Instead of wasting time marketing to a small proportion of people who might be interested, you're focusing on a group that's much more likely to interact with your content.

How Long Should You Promote a Webinar?

Three to four weeks is the ideal amount of time to promote your webinar. Any longer, you risk consumers not taking action or losing interest due to the extended wait period. On the other hand, a shorter promotion period may result in a poor turnout since fewer individuals are contacted and those who do not have enough time to organize. As the webinar's debut date approaches, you'll want to increase marketing to spread the news gradually. Webinar marketing is an excellent approach to get the attention of many individuals in your chosen area.

You may position your company as a leader and influencer in the area by providing something of value in the shape of a course or presentation. This technique has an influence that extends beyond the scope of the webinar and may be utilized as a part of a wider plan to establish your company as an expert. If you follow these webinar marketing best practices, you'll be on the right track. Bluehost offers the knowledge and tools to assist you in creating a website to support your webinar marketing.

Create a plan for your webinar

Did you know that Steve Jobs would practice his hour-long keynote speeches for hundreds of hours? Each of his major speeches had a schedule and a well-rehearsed script.

The audience for a small website owner will not be as large as that for an Apple keynote address. You may, however, acquire a vital lesson from Steve Jobs that will help you deliver better presentations.

Take the time to create a plan, a script, and rehearse it until it is flawless. Of course, you don't have to rehearse a one-hour speech for 100 hours, but having a plan and doing a few practice runs might assist.

Offer your products or services

Webinars are a great way to promote your products and services. Naturally, you don't want to start with a sales pitch, but it's a good idea to offer your products and services as an add-on towards the end of a webinar. For example, consider offering a limited-time discount or a unique promo code to your audience in exchange for attending the webinar. This gives additional motivation for participants to stay engaged with your brand.

Pick a webinar software or tool

You should choose a webinar software with a WordPress plugin before preparing your plan, but only after you have a general concept of what you want to accomplish. After that, what you choose will be determined by your needs, tastes, and whether or not it has the necessary integrations. Here are some characteristics of an excellent tool to look for:

- Allows for a minimum of two presenters.
- Unrestricted webinars
- Allows for at least 500 people to attend.
- Chat in real-time
- Reasonable time limits

- Functionality for recording
- WordPress incorporation
- Page creator
- Scheduling flexibility
- Email synchronization

Chapter-04: Benefits of hosting a webinar

The most obvious advantage of conducting a webinar at this period is that you can still do business without jeopardizing your own or your colleagues' or clients' health during the epidemic. But it isn't the only advantage. Even if we weren't amidst a global health crisis, conducting online webinars is a sound and profitable business strategy. Here are some of the most significant benefits of conducting a webinar.

You expand your reach

Although face-to-face meetings are an excellent method to develop connections, they are not the most convenient way to engage with your audience.

You or your clients must travel to meet in person. Traveling is costly, time-consuming, and inconvenient. Not to mention how tough it is to travel right now. You may easily connect with as many of your worldwide audience members as you desire if you conduct a webinar. All you need is a computer and a webinar software package to get started.

You establish authority in your industry

Even if you have years of expertise in your area, they are unlikely to think of you as the top industry leader if no one knows who you are.

You may fix this problem fast by holding informative webinars. Your followers will see you and your brand as a reliable source of knowledge as soon as they interact with you through webinars and hear your insightful and helpful thoughts.

You save money

Webinars are inexpensive. To run a successful webinar, all you need is an internet platform or plugin, a list of registrants, a webcam, a script, and some practice. Most professional webinar software solutions have everything you need to organize a successful webinar with a large audience. Furthermore, organizing a webinar is far less expensive than purchasing a plane ticket or planning a conference or in-person networking event.

You build brand awareness

When you conduct a webinar, you have hundreds of people paying attention. The audience not only gets to know you, but they also get over an hour of exposure to your brand. As you hold more webinars, your brand's visibility grows. The extra benefit is that when consumers have inquiries about your sector or are interested in a competitor's goods, guess who they will think of first? You and your company!

Webinars help you with market research

You most likely already have a general notion of who your target audience is. You could even have created a few client profiles. However, when you begin connecting with your audience online, you will have access to a wealth of comprehensive qualitative data. In other words, you find out what questions your target audience is asking. You discover what your consumers enjoy and dislike. You learn about their pain spots and how they feel about the competition.

Essentially, webinars allow you to ask questions and collect important information straight from your consumers, removing any guesswork from the equation. This information may be used to improve your content, adapt any of your existing products, and interact with your audience in more meaningful ways.

Webinars boost sales

Webinars are a great method to educate your audience while also increasing your reputation. They are also an excellent technique to increase revenue through product offers.

Many webinars provide instructional freebies followed by a brief commercial pitch. This approach is especially helpful for developing relationships and capturing more leads.

According to recent statistics, a single webinar may generate over 1,000 leads, and communication webinars have a conversion rate of more than 67 percent.

Steps to follow when planning a webinar

Now that you've learned about some of the most important advantages of holding a webinar let's go over everything you'll need to know to pull off a great event. Here are the procedures to take while organizing a webinar.

Get to know your audience

Before you select a date, choose a topic, or choose your speaker, you must first get to know your target audience better. Consider the following:

- What is the optimal client profile for me?
- What are my audience's concerns?

- What are my target audience's pain points?
- What is the greatest way for me to teach my audience?
- What are the interests of the audience?

The more you know about your target audience and what they want, the more effective your webinar. Therefore, consider conducting some market research or creating a more thorough client profile before choosing a topic.

Select your topic

It's time to pick a topic now that you've learned more about your audience. There are several approaches you may use when selecting a topic.

- Here are some things to think about:
- Investigate one of your most popular blog entries in further depth.
- Determine what information is lacking in your industry and address it.
- Does a Google search for popular queries about your business turn up any results?
- Answer questions from the audience and provide solutions.
- Free training on one of your business solutions is available.
- Teach your audience something they didn't know they did.'
- Use social media to poll your audience.

When choosing a topic, consider your blog statistics and customer data, and choose a topic that will resonate well with your audience.

Set a proper date and time for your webinar

This is a simple but crucial step. First, select a day and time that works best for your target audience. This involves taking into account schedules and time zones. For example, nobody wants to get up at 4 a.m. to attend a webinar.

Choose your webinar team

You may effectively hold your webinar if you are a one-person show. All it takes is a bit more planning and a fantastic webinar platform.

If you have a larger staff, it is a good idea to allocate particular duties. For example, consider delegating distinct tasks such as webinar organization, content creation, promotion, and presentation to separate individuals.

Determine the format of your webinar

Consider how many distinct presenting choices you have while attending an in-person conference. For example, one person may be heard speaking. You may listen to an interview. You can participate in a Q&A session or a panel discussion. Sometimes you'll encounter a combination of these distinct formats.

When running a webinar, you have the same set of options. However, your topic, team, audience, and network will determine the optimal webinar format.

Recruit speakers for your webinar

After you've settled on a topic, a time, a date, and a format, it's time to find speakers. You may either host the webinar yourself or invite a member of your team or an industry expert to present. When inviting someone to appear on your webinar, make sure you provide all the facts upfront.

Consider your webinar's design and visual branding

Remember how one of the primary advantages of having a webinar is increased brand recognition? It's true as long as you follow certain fundamental graphic design dos and don'ts.

Chapter-05: WordPress webinar plugins

WordPress plugins enable you to do almost everything you can think of with a website, including hosting webinars.

If you have a WordPress website, here are some of the best plugins to look into:

GoToWebinar – This is a dependable and user-friendly platform.

WebinarJam – This is one of the most popular services for hosting big webinars.

Webinars OnAir – This tool is great for remarketing and tracking the web activity of your consumers.

Google Hangouts – Google Hangouts may also be used to hold a webinar. However, you may be missing out on some of the more professional capabilities of a webinar platform.

Zoom – You've undoubtedly used Zoom for an online meeting, but you'll be pleased to discover that they also provide great webinar capability.

All of these platforms offer WordPress plugins that make doing a webinar on your WordPress site a breeze.

Ready to Host Your First Webinar?

Hosting a webinar is one of the finest methods to interact with your consumers, especially when meeting in person is impossible. Hosting a webinar will allow you to connect with your target audience, improve brand awareness, drive traffic back to your website, and encourage sales. If you're in the process of creating a WordPress website, don't forget to connect with the appropriate hosting company. HostGator provides outstanding WordPress hosting, shared hosting, and other services that may be suitable for your company. Check out HostGator right now.

How to create a perfect webinar

They help you connect with your audience, establish your authority as an expert, generate important leads, and increase sales. Without question, webinars are effective methods for promoting your company. Follow these ten simple steps to get the most of your online seminar!

Set your goals

First, consider why you're doing a webinar - is it to generate leads, establish your place in the business, or build your email list? Then, write out your objectives and keep them in mind while designing the webinar plan and selecting the best formula for your online seminar.

Follow the plan

Are you aware of your objectives? Great! You should now convert these into an easy-to-follow, step-by-step strategy for your webinar, as well as the project's timetable. When creating your to-do list, strive to be as precise as possible and avoid using general words such as "asking X to be a guest speaker." Instead, slice the cake by dividing your work down into little parts, such as "A. Google X's contact information. B. Send an invitation email." This technique will save you from feeling overwhelmed and allow you to track the progress of your project more efficiently.

Hit the perfect time

Time zones, national holidays, and the working style of your target audience are all important variables to consider when deciding on a day and time for your seminar. For example, midweek may be the best time to hold a webinar - Wednesdays and Thursdays have the greatest attendance rates, while Saturday and Sunday seminars have the lowest.

Not sure what time would be best for your target audience? Simply ask the poll participants and allow them to choose a day that will not conflict with their daily schedule. If you want a less direct approach to match the timing with your audience preferences, look at your Google Analytics data -

traffic peaks on your website may guide you to the ideal time for conducting your webinar.

Open for new audiences

How can you increase the number of people who attend your webinar? People who are already on your email list and are familiar with your company, in addition to inviting your main target, widen the audience. Reaching out to folks who have never heard of you and persuading them that your webinar offers unique value may be worth a shot! It simply takes the proper kind of marketing...

Spread the news

Behind every successful webinar is a well-planned advertising campaign. Plan a promotion strategy that includes detailed targeting and segmentation to help you reach the desired audience. Begin implementing your marketing approach at least two weeks before the event. The sooner you start, the more chances you'll have to capture the audience's attention and generate anticipation for your lecture.

Stick to the script

Do you want to know how to run a webinar like a pro? Even if you are completely prepared and enthusiastic about the subject, write down a script, which is essentially a comprehensive scenario that will structure your presentation, keep you on track, and prevent you from repeating material. The webinar script serves as a compass to lead you through your presentation and may also act as a "cheat sheet" on which you may rely in an emergency.

Be technically ready

And we mean it! You don't want to be concerned about technological difficulties as the webinar's host. Prepare the necessary software and gear, paying careful attention to audio and visual quality to provide your audience with a real-life experience. Consider providing technical assistance for yourself if you are the speaker. The existence of an assistant may save your webinar from a technological disaster and prevent you from worrying about whether your laptop will run out of juice.

Engage your audience

How can you engage your audience and retain their attention until the finish of your webinar? By merely connecting with them! Allow your visitors to voice their ideas and concerns, and invite them to share their experiences through a question and answer session. You may also encourage guests to participate in your social media channels by running a poll or starting a group chat.

Furthermore, reconsider how you display the facts - you may need to master your PowerPoint presentation. Instead of boring, static PowerPoint presentations, use dynamic images or charts to bring your slides to life.

Practice making it (almost) perfect

Rehearsals are necessary for live events such as webinars. Perform your pitch and test the equipment at least once before the final day. Even after you've practiced your speech numerous times, remember that there will always be circumstances beyond your control, but you can overcome any hurdles by being cool and cheerful.

Chapter-06: How to run global webinars?

Anyone who has ever been unable to attend a crucial meeting due to traffic or other unanticipated reasons understands how damaging such events can be to the entire notion of group work as well as the business itself. In today's fast-paced world, it is quite challenging to complete all of your tasks on time while being efficient and productive. Business owners required the proper solution, and it appears that developing webinars and expanding their popularity was the answer to many difficulties.

A webinar is a worldwide tool that connects people all over the world in a matter of seconds. It is an online presentation, or a real-time seminar, to which additional individuals may connect over the Internet. Webinars are also excellent for company promotion and may assist you in doing so more successfully, allowing your target audience to obtain all of the information they want faster and in real-time. It's also never been easier to collect leads.

Determine the purpose of your webinar

To properly begin designing a webinar, you must first establish the objective and ultimate aim of your presentation. For example, if you want to use a webinar to help your business grow, you might educate your visitors on using your product, display services, or even give training sessions.

Choosing which topics to discuss is also an important factor to consider. You'll be able to answer any of your audience's questions and clear up any misunderstandings. This is especially beneficial because it allows you to engage with your consumers directly. Once you've decided what you're going to deliver, it's time to tackle the technical aspects.

Understand what is required to launch a webinar

It is critical to address technological issues before joining the webinar room. Although there isn't much equipment required, there are a few necessities. A complete explanation on how to set up a home office can be found here, and however, in a nutshell, presenters must have the following:

- Webcam
- stable internet connection
- headset
- webinar hosting system

Similarly, the following items apply to attendees:

- headphones and microphone
- internet access

Now that we've covered the fundamental technical problems that must be addressed, we can move on to the webinar scheduling process. To begin a webinar, you must first schedule the event, which is a simple process. Create an account on a webinar platform and select a price plan first. When you first visit the website, you'll see a dashboard with many choices for scheduling webinars. Then, decide on a day for the webinar, the precise time it will begin, and how long the event will run - and you're done.

There are various ways to finish the registration procedure. You might, for example, send emails to all interested participants with a link to register for the webinar. To make the process as simple as possible, choose a webinar platform that integrates with email automation solutions, such as live webinars. After that, you may schedule messages to be sent to the recipients at the appropriate moment, such as sending a confirmation email to everyone who registered with a link to the event. Another option is to send an email with the webinar link the day before the presentation to remind them about it.

Ensure the addresses you send emails to are correct, which can be readily verified with email verification software.

Decide on your webinar's format

Depending on your objectives, you can hold a webinar by yourself or with a co-host. The most common alternatives are:

- A single presenter — one expert – offers some advice on a specific issue.
- Dual presenters are two specialists who share the stage.
- Panel - bring together a group of specialists to debate various issues and make things more interesting.

Product demonstration - as previously said, if you want to market your product or service, this is the ideal option for you. While having a guest speaker may be enjoyable for your audience, the process of contacting and selecting the perfect guest speaker may be time-consuming and tiring for you. You may use a combination of these forms or just one, but the most important thing is to discover the best method for your audience and what you intend to communicate to them.

Generate more leads

Lead generation may appear to be a difficult procedure, but it is rather simple. Everything you do and show on your website should be tailored to your target consumer. People should be able to learn more about your company by visiting your official website. It functions similarly to your identification card. Always strive to make your website understandable and informative to your visitors. Show them what you do, your aims, and where they can learn more about business, and so on.

It is also critical to demonstrate to them that you are available to them and that they may reach you at any moment. The simplest method to accomplish this is to create contact forms or use live chat on your website. You won't require much time to apply these; simply utilize website plugins, and your website will be optimized and user-friendly in a matter of minutes. When your target audience sees a genuine, competent staff behind your website, you will acquire more trust, and visitors will be more eager to join your webinars and learn more from you.

Increase website conversion rates

You have a far better chance of growing your email list and nurturing quality leads to become your future clients if you do worldwide webinars. The most effective approach to generating leads is to persuade them that you can fix their problems quickly and effectively. As a result, you must position your webinar as the finest answer customers can find online.

You may request their email addresses for them to participate in your webinar, and then when it is ready to begin, the user will be provided a link as a "ticket admission" to attend.

Many individuals do not go all the way to the bottom of a website, where contact forms are often placed on a page. As a result, you may infer that it is not the best location to invite people to your webinar. You should place this invitation in a much more obvious location.

Make your webinar more interactive

You were mistaken if you believed it was enough to sit in front of a computer and begin presenting an online presentation. It would help if you pictured everything as much as possible for your audience to comprehend your webinar topic fully. Using interactive technologies like desktop sharing to exhibit graphs, tables, images, and other media may elevate your presentation to the next level.

Keep it interesting by alternating between slides and formats and keeping their full attention while not confusing them. Use humor and narrative to make the entire experience more personal if you're talking about your brand, attempt to engage with your audience, and make an initial connection that will last or even strengthen as they become devoted consumers. To make your presentations more interesting, use a variety of media types. For example, polls and surveys offer the appearance that you value your listeners' opinions, which makes you feel good and supplies you with potentially helpful input.

Practice makes perfect

A webinar is seldom complete without at least some minor interruption. That is why you must be prepared for everything and prepare well. It is recommended to perform a trial webinar to decrease the risk of problems occurring. Test your speakers and make sure you sound clear using the webinar program of your choice. Of course, it is not enough for your speakers to operate to be heard loud and clear; you must also pronounce effectively and utter succinct phrases. In addition, you must make your speech engaging and simple to follow.

You should take notes, but you may also be more flexible and spontaneous on occasion since this differentiates an ordinary webinar from a high-quality one.

Conclusion

Because individuals have less time to attend meetings and accomplish many tasks simultaneously, webinars or online seminars are becoming increasingly popular. In addition, individuals grew interested in webinars when they discovered they could use them to advertise their businesses and reach a bigger number of potential consumers. Thus, this became an excellent method for increasing conversion rates. We stated a few suggestions for doing a worldwide webinar, and if you follow them, you will be on the right route.

Webinars may be utilized for a variety of reasons. For example, you might provide your visitors with a tutorial demonstrating your service, or you could describe your product in a nutshell yet successful enough to increase conversions and purchases. Lead generation is a time-consuming procedure, but it is well worth the effort.

www.ingramcontent.com/pod-product-compliance
Lightning Source LLC
Chambersburg PA
CBHW030038230526
45472CB00002B/569